Contents

CROCK-POT® SLOW

Stirring

Due to the nature of slow cooking, there is no need to stir the food unless the recipe method says to do so. In fact, taking the lid off to stir food causes your **CROCK-POT®** slow cooker to lose a significant amount of heat, which extends the cooking time required. Therefore, it is best not to remove the lid for stirring.

Adding Ingredients at the End of the Cooking Time

Certain ingredients are best added toward the end of the cooking time. These include:
- Milk, sour cream, and yogurt: Add during the last 15 minutes.
- Seafood and fish: Add during the last 15 to 30 minutes.
- Fresh herbs: Fresh herbs such as basil will darken with long cooking, so if you want colorful fresh herbs, add those during the last 15 minutes of cooking time or directly to the dish just before serving it.

Pasta and Rice

For slow-cooked rice dishes, converted rice holds up best through longer cooking times. Most recipes suggest adding pasta or rice halfway through the cooking time for the best texture. If the rice doesn't seem completely cooked after the suggested time, add an extra ½ cup to 1 cup of liquid per cup of rice, and extend the cooking time by 30 to 60 minutes.

Cooking With Frozen Foods

You may cook frozen foods in your **CROCK-POT®** slow cooker. For best results, use the following guidelines:
- Add at least 1 cup of warm or hot liquid to the stoneware before placing frozen meat in the **CROCK-POT®** slow cooker.
- Do not preheat the **CROCK-POT®** slow cooker.
- Cook recipes containing frozen meats for an additional 4 to 6 hours on LOW or 2 hours on HIGH.
- Slow-cooking frozen foods requires a longer cook time than fresh foods because it will take longer for the food to come up to safe internal temperatures. Meats also will require additional time to allow them to become tender. If there is any question about the cooking time, use a thermometer to ensure meats are cooking appropriately.

Cooking Temperatures and Food Safety

Cooking meats in your **CROCK-POT®** slow cooker is perfectly safe. According to the U.S. Department of Agriculture, bacteria in food is killed at a temperature of 165°F. As a result, it's important to follow the recommended cooking times, and to keep the cover on your **CROCK-POT®** slow cooker during the cooking process to maintain food-safe temperatures. Slow-cooked meats and poultry are best when simmered gently for the period of time that allows connective tissues to break down, yielding meat that is fall-off-the-bone tender and juicy.

COOKER
Hints and Tips

Browning Meat

Meat will not brown as it would if it were
cooked in a skillet or oven at a high temperature.
It is not necessary to brown meat before slow
cooking. However, if you prefer the flavor
and look of browned meat, just brown it in
a large skillet coated with oil, butter or
nonstick cooking oil, then place the
browned ingredients into the stoneware
and follow the recipe as written.

Herbs and Spices

When cooking with your
CROCK-POT® slow cooker, use
dried and ground herbs and spices,
which work well during long cook times.
However, the flavor and aroma of
crushed or ground herbs differ depending
on their shelf life, and their flavor can lessen
during an extended cooking time. Be sure to taste
the finished dish and add more seasonings if needed. If
you prefer colorful fresh herbs, add them during the last
15 minutes of cooking time or to the dish as a garnish.

Cooking for Larger Quantity Yields

If you want to make a bigger batch in a larger unit, such as a 5-, 6-, or
7-quart **CROCK-POT®** slow cooker, guidelines for doubling or tripling
ingredients include:

- When preparing dishes with beef or pork in a larger unit, browning the
  meat in a skillet before adding it to the **CROCK-POT®** slow cooker
  yields the best results; the meat will cook more evenly.
- Roasted meats, chicken, and turkey quantities may be doubled or tripled,
  and seasonings adjusted by half. Caution: Flavorful dried spices such as
  garlic and chili powder will intensify during long slow cooking. Add just
  25 to 50 percent more spices as needed to balance the flavors.
- When preparing a soup or a stew, you may double all the ingredients
  except the liquids, seasonings, and dried herbs. Increase the liquid volume
  by half, or adjust as needed. The **CROCK-POT®** slow cooker lid collects
  steam, which condenses to keep foods moist and maintain liquid volume.
- Do not double thickeners, such as cornstarch, at the beginning. You may
  always add more thickener later if it's necessary.
- When preparing baked goods or cheesecakes, it is best to simply prepare
  the original recipe as many times as needed to serve more people.

MEXICAN
COCINA

Easy Taco Dip

MAKES ABOUT 3 CUPS DIP

PREP TIME: 10 TO 15 MINUTES
COOK TIME: 2 TO 4 HOURS (LOW) • 1 TO 2 HOURS (HIGH)

½	**pound ground chuck**
1	**cup frozen corn**
½	**cup chopped onion**
½	**cup salsa**
½	**cup mild taco sauce**
1	**can (4 ounces) diced mild green chilies**
1	**can (4 ounces) sliced ripe olives, drained**
1	**cup (4 ounces) shredded Mexican cheese blend**
	Tortilla chips
	Sour cream

1. Cook meat in large nonstick skillet until no longer pink, stirring to separate; drain. Spoon into **CROCK-POT**® slow cooker.

2. Add corn, onion, salsa, taco sauce, chilies and olives to **CROCK-POT**® slow cooker; stir to combine. Cover and cook on LOW 2 to 4 hours or on HIGH 1 to 2 hours or until done.

3. Just before serving, stir in cheese. Serve with tortilla chips and sour cream.

Tip: To keep this dip hot while serving at your party, simply leave it in the **CROCK-POT**® slow cooker on LOW.

Chicken Enchilada Roll-Ups

MAKES 6 SERVINGS

PREP TIME: 20 MINUTES
COOK TIME: 7 TO 8 HOURS (LOW) • 3 TO 4 HOURS (HIGH)

1½	pounds boneless skinless chicken breasts
½	cup plus 2 tablespoons all-purpose flour, divided
½	teaspoon salt
2	tablespoons butter
1	cup chicken broth
1	small onion, diced
¼	to ½ cup canned jalapeño peppers, sliced
½	teaspoon dried oregano
2	tablespoons cream or milk
6	flour tortillas (7 to 8 inches)
6	thin slices American cheese or American cheese with jalapeño peppers

1. Cut each chicken breast lengthwise into 2 or 3 strips. Combine ½ cup flour and salt in resealable plastic food storage bag. Add chicken strips and shake to coat with flour mixture. Melt butter in large skillet over medium heat. Remove chicken from bag and shake off excess flour. Brown chicken strips in batches 2 to 3 minutes per side. Place chicken into **CROCK-POT®** slow cooker.

2. Add chicken broth to skillet and stir in any browned bits. Pour broth mixture into **CROCK-POT®** slow cooker. Add onion, jalapeño peppers and oregano. Cover and cook on LOW 7 to 8 hours or on HIGH 3 to 4 hours or until done.

3. Combine remaining 2 tablespoons of flour and cream in small bowl; stir to form paste. Stir into chicken mixture; cook on HIGH until thickened.

4. Spoon chicken mixture in center of flour tortilla. Top with 1 cheese slice; repeat. Fold up tortillas and serve.

Campbell's® Mexican Beef & Bean Stew

MAKES 6 SERVINGS

PREP TIME: 10 MINUTES
COOK TIME: 8 TO 10 HOURS (LOW) • 4 TO 5 HOURS (HIGH)

1½	**pounds beef for stew, cut into 1-inch cubes**
2	**tablespoons all-purpose flour**
1	**tablespoon vegetable oil**
1	**cup coarsely chopped onion**
1	**can (about 15 ounces) pinto beans**
1	**can (about 15 ounces) whole kernel corn, drained**
1	**can Campbell's® Condensed Beef Consommé**
1	**cup Pace® Chunky Salsa**
2	**tablespoons chili powder**
1	**teaspoon ground cumin**
¼	**teaspoon garlic powder or 2 cloves garlic, minced**

1. Coat beef with flour. Heat oil in skillet. Add beef and cook until browned.

2. Place beef, onion, beans, corn, consommé, salsa, chili powder, cumin and garlic in the **CROCK-POT®** slow cooker.

3. Cover and cook on LOW for 8 to 10 hours or on HIGH for 4 to 5 hours or until done.

Campbell's Is Cooking With Crock-Pot®!

Opening the lid and checking on food in the slow cooker can affect both cooking time and results. Due to the nature of slow cooking, there is no need to stir the food unless the recipe method says to do so.

Layered Mexican-Style Casserole

MAKES 6 SERVINGS

PREP TIME: 15 MINUTES
COOK TIME: 6 TO 8 HOURS (LOW) • 2 TO 3 HOURS (HIGH)

2 **cans (15½ ounces each) hominy, drained**
1 **can (15 ounces) black beans, rinsed and drained**
1 **can (14½ ounces) diced tomatoes with garlic, basil and oregano, undrained**
1 **cup chunky salsa**
1 **can (6 ounces) tomato paste**
½ **teaspoon ground cumin**
3 **large (about 9-inch diameter) flour tortillas**
2 **cups (8 ounces) shredded Monterey Jack cheese**
¼ **cup sliced black olives**

1. Prepare foil handles (see below). Spray **CROCK-POT**® slow cooker stoneware with nonstick cooking spray.

2. Stir together hominy, beans, tomatoes with juice, salsa, tomato paste and cumin in a large bowl.

3. Press 1 tortilla in the bottom of **CROCK-POT**® slow cooker. (Edges of tortilla may turn up slightly.) Top with ⅓ of hominy mixture and ⅓ of cheese. Repeat layers. Press remaining tortilla on top. Top with remaining hominy mixture. Set aside remaining cheese.

4. Cover and cook on LOW 6 to 8 hours or on HIGH 2 to 3 hours or until done. Sprinkle with remaining cheese and olives. Cover, turn off heat, and let stand 5 minutes. Lift out stacked tortilla casserole with foil handles.

Note: Hominy can be found with the canned vegetables in most supermarkets.

Foil handles: Tear off three 18×2-inch strips of heavy foil or use regular foil folded to double thickness. Crisscross foil strips in spoke design and place into **CROCK-POT**® slow cooker. Center the base layer of tortilla on top of the center of the spoke design. Press foil handles up against the edge of the stoneware crock, and continue layering casserole ingredients. When the casserole has cooked and cooled, hold the foil strips to make lifting the tortilla stack easier.

Mexican Chili Chicken

MAKES 4 SERVINGS

PREP TIME: 10 MINUTES
COOK TIME: 7 TO 8 HOURS (LOW) • 2 TO 3 HOURS (HIGH)

2	medium green bell peppers, cut into thin strips
1	large onion, quartered and thinly sliced
4	chicken thighs
4	chicken drumsticks
1	tablespoon chili powder
2	teaspoons dried oregano
1	jar (16 ounces) chipotle salsa
½	cup ketchup
2	teaspoons ground cumin
½	teaspoon salt
	Hot cooked noodles

1. Place bell peppers and onion in **CROCK-POT**® slow cooker; top with chicken. Sprinkle chili powder and oregano evenly over chicken. Add salsa. Cover and cook on LOW 7 to 8 hours or on HIGH 2 to 3 hours or until chicken is tender.

2. Transfer chicken pieces to serving bowl; keep warm. Stir ketchup, cumin and salt into cooking liquid in **CROCK-POT**® slow cooker. Cook, uncovered, on HIGH 15 minutes or until hot.

3. Pour mixture over chicken. Serve with noodles.

Tip: For thicker sauce, blend together 1 tablespoon cornstarch and 2 tablespoons water. Stir into cooking liquid with ketchup, cumin and salt.

Campbell's® Nacho Chicken & Rice Wraps

MAKES 10 SERVINGS

PREP TIME: 5 MINUTES
COOK TIME: 7 TO 8 HOURS (LOW) • 4 TO 5 HOURS (HIGH)

2	**cans Campbell's® Cheddar Cheese Soup**
1	**cup water**
2	**cups Pace® Chunky Salsa or Picante Sauce**
1¼	**cups uncooked regular long-grain white rice**
2	**pounds boneless chicken breasts, cubed**
10	**flour tortillas (10 inches in diameter)**

1. Mix soup, water, salsa, rice and chicken in the **CROCK-POT®** slow cooker. Cover and cook on LOW for 7 to 8 hours or on HIGH for 4 to 5 hours or until done.

2. Spoon about 1 cup rice mixture down center of each tortilla. Fold tortilla around filling.

Tip: For firmer rice, substitute converted rice for regular long-grain rice.

Corn and Beans

MAKES 6 SERVINGS

PREP TIME: 15 MINUTES
COOK TIME: 7 TO 8 HOURS (LOW) • 2 TO 3 HOURS (HIGH)

1	tablespoon olive oil
1	large onion, diced
1	or 2 jalapeño peppers,* diced
1	clove garlic, minced
2	cans (16 ounces) light red kidney beans, rinsed and drained
1	bag (16 ounces) frozen corn
1	can (14½ ounces) diced tomatoes, undrained
1	green bell pepper, cut into 1-inch pieces
2	teaspoons medium-hot chili powder
¾	teaspoon salt
½	teaspoon ground cumin
½	teaspoon black pepper
1	carton (8 ounces) plain yogurt (optional)
	Sliced black olives (optional)

*Jalapeño peppers can sting and irritate the skin; wear rubber gloves when handling peppers and do not touch eyes. Wash hands after handling.

1. Heat oil in medium skillet. Add onion, jalapeño pepper and garlic; cook 5 minutes. Add onion mixture, beans, corn, tomatoes with juice, bell pepper, chili powder, salt, cumin and black pepper to **CROCK-POT®** slow cooker. Cover and cook on LOW 7 to 8 hours or on HIGH 2 to 3 hours or until done.

2. Spoon corn and beans into bowls. Serve with yogurt and black olives, if desired.

Tip: For a party, spoon this colorful vegetarian dish into hollowed-out bread bowls.

Three-Bean Mole Chili

MAKES 4 TO 6 SERVINGS

PREP TIME: 10 MINUTES
COOK TIME: 5 TO 6 HOURS (LOW) • 1 TO 2 HOURS (HIGH)

1   can (15 ounces) pinto beans, rinsed and drained
1   can (15 ounces) chili beans in spicy sauce, undrained
1   can (15 ounces) black beans, rinsed and drained
1   can (14½ ounces) Mexican or chili-style diced tomatoes, undrained
1   large green bell pepper, diced
1   small onion, diced
½   cup beef, chicken or vegetable broth
¼   cup prepared mole paste*
2   teaspoons ground cumin
2   teaspoons ground coriander (optional)
2   teaspoons chili powder
2   teaspoons minced garlic
    Crushed tortilla chips (optional)
    Chopped cilantro (optional)
    Shredded cheese (optional)

*Mole paste is available in the Mexican food section of large supermarkets or in specialty markets.

1. Combine beans, tomatoes with juice, bell pepper, onion, broth, mole paste, cumin, coriander, if desired, chili powder and garlic in the **CROCK-POT®** slow cooker; mix well.

2. Cover and cook on LOW 5 to 6 hours or on HIGH 1 to 2 hours or until vegetables are tender.

3. Serve with chips, cilantro or cheese, if desired.

Black Bean-Stuffed Peppers

MAKES 6 SERVINGS

PREP TIME: 15 MINUTES
COOK TIME: 6 TO 8 HOURS (LOW) • 3 TO 4 HOURS (HIGH)

1	medium onion, peeled and finely chopped
¼	teaspoon ground red pepper
¼	teaspoon dried oregano
¼	teaspoon ground cumin
¼	teaspoon chili powder
1	can (15 ounces) black beans, rinsed and drained, divided
6	tall green bell peppers, tops removed, seeded and cored
1	cup reduced-fat Monterey Jack cheese, grated
1	cup tomato salsa
½	cup fat-free sour cream

1. Coat medium skillet with nonstick cooking spray. Add onion and cook over medium heat until golden. Add red pepper, oregano, cumin and chili powder.

2. Mash half of black beans with cooked onions in medium mixing bowl. Stir in remaining beans. Place bell peppers in **CROCK-POT**® slow cooker, and spoon black bean mixture into bell peppers. Sprinkle cheese over peppers. Pour salsa over cheese. Cover and cook on LOW 6 to 8 hours or on HIGH 3 to 4 hours or until done.

3. Serve each pepper with dollop of sour cream.

Crock∗Pot®
Stoneware Slow Cooker

Spicy Tex-Mex Bowl

MAKES 8 TO 10 SERVINGS

PREP TIME: 35 MINUTES
COOK TIME: 5 TO 6 HOURS (LOW) • 3 TO 4 HOURS (HIGH)

⅓	cup lentils, uncooked
1⅓	cups water
5	strips bacon
1	onion, chopped
1	can (16 ounces) pinto beans, undrained
1	can (16 ounces) red kidney beans, undrained
1	can (15 ounces) diced tomatoes, undrained
3	tablespoons ketchup
3	cloves garlic, minced
1	teaspoon chili powder
½	teaspoon ground cumin
¼	teaspoon red pepper flakes
1	bay leaf

1. Boil lentils in water 20 to 30 minutes in large saucepan; drain.

2. Cook bacon until crisp in small skillet; drain and crumble bacon. In same skillet, cook onion in bacon drippings until soft.

3. Combine lentils, bacon, onion, beans with juice, tomatoes with juice, ketchup, garlic, chili powder, cumin, pepper flakes and bay leaf in **CROCK-POT**® slow cooker. Cook on LOW 5 to 6 hours or on HIGH 3 to 4 hours or until done. Remove bay leaf before serving.

ITALIAN CUCINA

Tarragon Turkey & Pasta

MAKES 4 SERVINGS

PREP TIME: 15 TO 20 MINUTES
COOK TIME: 6 TO 8 HOURS (LOW) • 3½ TO 4 HOURS (HIGH)

1½	to 2 pounds turkey tenderloins
¼	cup dry white wine
½	cup thinly sliced celery
¼	cup thinly sliced green onions
4	tablespoons minced fresh tarragon, divided
1	teaspoon salt
1	teaspoon black pepper
½	cup plain yogurt
2	tablespoons minced fresh Italian parsley
2	tablespoons lemon juice
1½	tablespoons cornstarch
2	tablespoons water
4	cups pasta of your choice, cooked al dente

1. Combine turkey, wine, celery, green onions, 2 tablespoons tarragon, salt and pepper in **CROCK-POT**® slow cooker; mix thoroughly. Cover and cook on LOW 6 to 8 hours or on HIGH 3½ to 4 hours or until done.

2. Remove cooked turkey from **CROCK-POT**® slow cooker, and cut into ½-inch-thick medallions. Turn **CROCK-POT**® slow cooker to HIGH. Add yogurt, remaining tarragon, parsley and lemon juice to cooking liquid.

3. Combine cornstarch and water in small bowl. Add to **CROCK-POT**® slow cooker and cook until cooking liquid thickens. Serve turkey medallions over pasta. Drizzle with tarragon sauce.

Three-Pepper Pasta Sauce

MAKES 4 TO 6 SERVINGS

PREP TIME: 10 TO 15 MINUTES
COOK TIME: 7 TO 8 HOURS (LOW) ● 3 TO 4 HOURS (HIGH)

1	red bell pepper, cut into 1-inch pieces
1	green bell pepper, cut into 1-inch pieces
1	yellow bell pepper, cut into 1-inch pieces
2	cans (14½ ounces each) diced tomatoes, undrained
1	cup chopped onion
1	can (6 ounces) tomato paste
4	cloves garlic, minced
2	tablespoons olive oil
1	teaspoon dried basil
1	teaspoon dried oregano
½	teaspoon salt
¼	teaspoon red pepper flakes or ground black pepper
	Hot cooked pasta of your choice
	Shredded Parmesan or Romano cheese

1. Combine bell peppers, tomatoes with juice, onion, tomato paste, garlic, oil, basil, oregano, salt and red pepper flakes in **CROCK-POT®** slow cooker. Cover and cook on LOW 7 to 8 hours or on HIGH 3 to 4 hours or until vegetables are tender.

2. Adjust seasonings, if desired. Serve with pasta and garnish with cheese.

Tip: Save time by purchasing 3 cups mixed bell pepper chunks from supermarket or deli salad bar.

Italian-Style Sausage with Rice

MAKES 4 TO 5 SERVINGS

PREP TIME: 10 TO 15 MINUTES
COOK TIME: 4 TO 6 HOURS (LOW) • 2 TO 3 HOURS (HIGH)

1	pound mild Italian sausage, cut into 1-inch pieces
1	can (29 ounces) pinto beans, rinsed and drained
1	cup spaghetti sauce
1	green bell pepper, cut into strips
1	small onion, halved and sliced
½	teaspoon salt
¼	teaspoon black pepper
	Hot cooked rice
	Chopped fresh basil (optional)

1. Brown sausage in large nonstick skillet. Pour off drippings.

2. Place sausage, beans, spaghetti sauce, bell pepper, onion, salt and pepper into **CROCK-POT®** slow cooker. Cover; cook on LOW 4 to 6 hours or on HIGH 2 to 3 hours or until done.

3. Serve with rice. Garnish with basil, if desired.

Campbell's® Tuscan Beef Stew

MAKES 8 SERVINGS

PREP TIME: 5 TO 10 MINUTES
COOK TIME: 8 TO 9 HOURS (LOW) • 4 TO 5 HOURS (HIGH)

- 1   can (10¾ ounces) Campbell's® Tomato Soup
- 1   can Campbell's® Condensed Beef Broth
- ½   cup red wine or water
- 2   pounds beef stew meat, cut into 1-inch pieces
- 1   can (14½ ounces) diced Italian-style tomatoes
- 3   large carrots, cut into 1-inch pieces
- 1   teaspoon Italian seasoning, crushed
- ½   teaspoon garlic powder
- 2   cans (about 16 ounces each) white kidney (cannellini) beans, drained

1. Mix soup, broth, wine, beef, tomatoes, carrots, Italian seasoning and garlic powder in the **CROCK-POT®** slow cooker.

2. Cover and cook on LOW for 8 to 9 hours or on HIGH for 4 to 5 hours or until done.

3. Stir in beans. Turn heat to HIGH and cook 10 minutes.

Herbed Artichoke Chicken

MAKES 6 SERVINGS

PREP TIME: 5 MINUTES
COOK TIME: 6 TO 8 HOURS (LOW) ● **3½ TO 4 HOURS (HIGH)**

1½	**pounds skinless, boneless chicken breasts**
1	**can (14 ounces) tomatoes, drained and diced**
1	**can (14 ounces) artichoke hearts in water, drained**
1	**small onion, chopped**
½	**cup kalamata olives, pitted and sliced**
1	**cup nonfat chicken broth**
¼	**cup dry white wine**
1	**tablespoon quick-cooking tapioca**
1	**teaspoon curry powder**
1	**tablespoon chopped fresh Italian parsley**
1	**teaspoon dried sweet basil**
1	**teaspoon dried thyme**
½	**teaspoon salt**
½	**teaspoon freshly ground black pepper**

1. Combine chicken, tomatoes, artichokes, onion, olives, broth, wine, tapioca, curry powder, parsley, basil, thyme, salt and pepper in **CROCK-POT**® slow cooker. Mix thoroughly.

2. Cover and cook on LOW 6 to 8 hours or on HIGH 3½ to 4 hours or until done.

Swanson® Chicken Cacciatore

MAKES 6 SERVINGS

PREP TIME: 10 MINUTES
COOK TIME: 7 TO 8 HOURS (LOW) • 4 TO 5 HOURS (HIGH)

3	pounds chicken parts, skin removed
1	can (14 ounces) Swanson® Chicken Broth or Natural Goodness™ Chicken Broth (1¾ cups)
2	cans (14½ ounces each) diced Italian-style tomatoes
4	cups mushrooms cut in half
2	large onions, chopped
1	teaspoon garlic powder
10	cups hot cooked spaghetti

1. Place chicken in the **CROCK-POT®** slow cooker. Add broth, tomatoes, mushrooms, onions and garlic.

2. Cover and cook on LOW for 7 to 8 hours or on HIGH for 4 to 5 hours or until done. Serve over spaghetti.

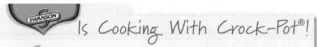

Is Cooking With Crock-Pot®!

For thicker sauce, mix together 2 tablespoons cornstarch and 2 tablespoons water. Remove chicken from stoneware. Stir cornstarch mixture into stoneware. Cover and cook on HIGH for 10 minutes or until mixture thickens.

Campbell's® Zesty Italian Pot Roast

MAKES 4 TO 6 SERVINGS

PREP TIME: 10 MINUTES
COOK TIME: 10 TO 12 HOURS (LOW) • 4 TO 6 HOURS (HIGH)

4   medium potatoes, quartered (about 4 cups)
2   cups fresh or frozen baby carrots
1   stalk celery, cut in 1-inch pieces
½   cup diced plum tomato
1   (2½-pound) boneless beef chuck roast
½   teaspoon black pepper
1   can (10¾ ounces) Campbell's® Tomato Soup
½   cup water
1   tablespoon roasted garlic*
1   teaspoon dried basil
1   teaspoon dried oregano
1   teaspoon dried parsley flakes, crushed
1   teaspoon vinegar

*To roast garlic, place whole garlic bulb on piece of aluminum foil. Drizzle with a little oil and wrap. Roast in oven at 350°F for 45 minutes or until soft.

1. Place potatoes, carrots, celery and tomato in the **CROCK-POT®** slow cooker. Season roast with pepper and place on top of vegetables.

2. Mix together soup, water, garlic, basil, oregano, parsley and vinegar. Pour over meat and vegetables in stoneware.

3. Cover and cook on LOW for 10 to 12 hours or on HIGH for 4 to 6 hours or until done.

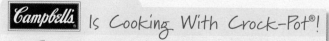

Campbell's Is Cooking With Crock-Pot®!

For thicker gravy, mix ¼ cup all-purpose flour with ½ cup water. Remove beef from stoneware. Add flour mixture to stoneware. Turn heat to HIGH. Cook until mixture thickens, about 10 minutes.

WINTER WARMERS

Wild Mushroom Beef Stew

MAKES 5 SERVINGS

PREP TIME: 15 TO 20 MINUTES
COOK TIME: 10 TO 12 HOURS (LOW) • 4 HOURS (HIGH)

- 1½ to 2 pounds beef stew meat, cut into 1-inch cubes
- ⅛ cup flour
- ½ teaspoon salt
- ½ teaspoon black pepper
- 1½ cups beef broth
- 1 teaspoon Worcestershire sauce
- 1 clove garlic, minced
- 1 bay leaf
- 1 teaspoon paprika
- 4 shiitake mushrooms,* sliced
- 2 medium carrots, sliced
- 2 medium potatoes, diced
- 1 small white onion, chopped
- 1 stalk celery, sliced

*If shiitake mushrooms are unavailable, substitute other mushrooms of your choice. For extra punch, add a few dried porcini mushrooms.

1. Put beef in **CROCK-POT®** slow cooker. Mix together flour, salt and pepper, and pour over meat; stir to coat each piece of meat with flour. Add remaining ingredients and stir to mix well.

2. Cover and cook on LOW 10 to 12 hours or on HIGH 4 hours or until done. Stir stew before serving.

WINTER WARMERS

McCormick® Beef Stew

MAKES 6 SERVINGS

PREP TIME: 15 MINUTES
COOK TIME: 7 TO 8 HOURS (LOW) • 5 HOURS (HIGH)

5   cups fresh chopped stew vegetables (potatoes, carrots, onions, celery)
3   cups water
1   package McCormick® Beef Stew Seasoning
2   pounds beef chuck or stew meat, cut into 1-inch cubes
¼   cup flour

1. Combine vegetables, water and seasoning in the **CROCK-POT®** slow cooker. Coat beef with flour and stir into ingredients in stoneware.

2. Cook on LOW for 7 to 8 hours or HIGH for 5 hours or until beef is tender.

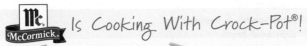

Is Cooking With Crock-Pot®!

For faster cooking time and more tender beef, brown the flour-coated beef in 2 tablespoons olive oil in a large skillet placed over medium heat. Drain, and then add the browned beef to the remaining ingredients in the **CROCK-POT®** slow cooker. Cook on HIGH for 4 hours or until tender.

Chicken Provencal

MAKES 8 SERVINGS

PREP TIME: 15 TO 20 MINUTES
COOK TIME: 7 TO 9 HOURS (LOW) • 3 TO 4 HOURS (HIGH)

2	pounds skinless boneless chicken thighs, each cut into quarters
2	medium red bell peppers, cut into ¼-inch thick slices
1	medium yellow bell pepper, cut into ¼-inch thick slices
1	onion, thinly sliced
1	can (28 ounces) plum tomatoes, drained
3	cloves garlic, minced
¼	teaspoon salt
¼	teaspoon thyme
¼	teaspoon fennel seeds, crushed
3	strips orange peel
½	cup chopped fresh basil

1. Place chicken, bell peppers, onion, tomatoes, garlic, salt, thyme, fennel seeds and orange peel in **CROCK-POT®** slow cooker. Mix thoroughly.

2. Cover and cook on LOW 7 to 9 hours or on HIGH 3 to 4 hours or until done.

3. Sprinkle with basil to serve.

Note: Serve with a crusty French baguette and seasonal vegetables.

Swanson® Slow-Simmered Chicken Rice Soup

MAKES 8 SERVINGS

PREP TIME: 15 MINUTES
COOK TIME: 7 TO 8 HOURS (LOW) • 4 TO 5 HOURS (HIGH)

½   **cup uncooked wild rice**
½   **cup uncooked regular long-grain white rice**
1   **tablespoon vegetable oil**
1   **medium onion, chopped**
2   **stalks celery, coarsely chopped**
1   **pound boneless chicken breasts, cut up**
2   **teaspoons dried thyme leaves, crushed**
¼   **teaspoon crushed red pepper**
3   **cans (14 ounces each) Swanson® Chicken Broth or Natural Goodness™ Chicken Broth (5¼ cups)**

1. Mix wild rice, white rice and oil in the **CROCK-POT®** slow cooker. Cover and cook on HIGH 15 minutes.

2. Stir in onion, celery, chicken, thyme, pepper and broth. Cover and cook on LOW for 7 to 8 hours or on HIGH for 4 to 5 hours or until done.

3. Serve with sour cream and green onions, if desired.

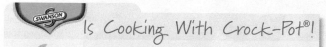

Is Cooking With Crock-Pot®!

Speed preparation by substituting 3 (5-ounce) cans **Swanson® Premium Chunk Chicken** instead of the raw poultry.

Parsnip and Carrot Soup

MAKES 4 SERVINGS

PREP TIME: 15 MINUTES
COOK TIME: 6 TO 9 HOURS (LOW) • 2 TO 4 HOURS (HIGH)

1	medium leek, thinly sliced
4	medium parsnips, peeled and diced
4	medium carrots, peeled and diced
4	cups fat-free chicken stock
1	bay leaf
½	teaspoon salt
½	teaspoon freshly ground black pepper
½	cup small pasta, cooked al dente and drained
1	tablespoon chopped Italian parsley
1	cup low-fat croutons

1. Coat medium skillet with nonstick cooking spray. Add leek and cook over medium heat until golden. Place in **CROCK-POT®** slow cooker.

2. Add parsnips, carrots, stock, bay leaf, salt and pepper. Cover and cook on LOW 6 to 9 hours or on HIGH 2 to 4 hours or until vegetables are tender.

3. Add pasta during last hour of cooking. Sprinkle each individual serving with parsley and croutons.

Note: This dish is a great year-round accompaniment to roasted meats, or can stand alone as a satisfying soup.

Chicken and Sweet Potato Stew

MAKES 6 SERVINGS

PREP TIME: 15 MINUTES
COOK TIME: 6 TO 8 HOURS (LOW) • 3 TO 4 HOURS (HIGH)

4	boneless skinless chicken breasts, cut into bite-sized pieces
2	medium sweet potatoes, peeled and cubed
2	medium Yukon Gold potatoes, peeled and cubed
2	medium carrots, peeled and cut into ½-inch slices
1	can (28 ounces) whole stewed tomatoes
1	teaspoon salt
½	teaspoon freshly ground black pepper
¼	teaspoon ground cinnamon
¼	teaspoon ground nutmeg
1	teaspoon paprika
1	teaspoon celery seed
1	cup fat-free low-sodium chicken broth
¼	cup chopped fresh basil

1. Combine chicken, potatoes, carrots, tomatoes, salt, pepper, cinnamon, nutmeg, paprika, celery seed and broth in **CROCK-POT**® slow cooker.

2. Cover and cook on LOW 6 to 8 hours or on HIGH 3 to 4 hours or until done.

3. Sprinkle with basil just before serving.

Asian FLAVORS

Asian-Spiced Chicken Wings

MAKES 10 TO 16 WINGS

PREP TIME: 20 TO 25 MINUTES
COOK TIME: 5 TO 6 HOURS (LOW) ● 2 TO 3 HOURS (HIGH)

3	**pounds chicken wings**
1	**cup soy sauce**
1	**cup packed brown sugar**
½	**cup ketchup**
1	**teaspoon fresh ginger, minced**
1	**clove garlic, minced**
¼	**cup dry sherry**
½	**cup hoisin sauce**
1	**tablespoon fresh lime juice**
2	**tablespoons sesame seeds, toasted**
¼	**cup green onions, thinly sliced**

1. Preheat broiler. Place chicken wings on broiler pan. Broil 4 to 5 inches from heat 10 minutes per side, or until wings are brown. Transfer to **CROCK-POT®** slow cooker.

2. Add soy sauce, brown sugar, ketchup, ginger, garlic and sherry; stir thoroughly to coat wings. Cover and cook on LOW 5 to 6 hours or on HIGH 2 to 3 hours or until chicken wings are no longer pink, stirring once halfway through cooking time to baste wings with sauce.

3. Remove wings from **CROCK-POT®** slow cooker. Reserve ¼ cup of cooking liquid; combine with hoisin sauce and lime juice. Drizzle mixture over wings. Sprinkle with sesame seeds and green onions before serving.

Simmering Hot & Sour Soup

MAKES 4 SERVINGS

PREP TIME: 10 TO 15 MINUTES
COOK TIME: 3 TO 4 HOURS (LOW) • 2 TO 3 HOURS (HIGH)

2	cans (14½ ounces each) chicken broth
1	cup chopped cooked chicken or pork
4	ounces fresh shiitake mushroom caps, thinly sliced
½	cup sliced bamboo shoots, cut into thin strips
3	tablespoons rice wine vinegar
2	tablespoons soy sauce
1½	teaspoons chili paste or 1 teaspoon hot chili oil
4	ounces firm tofu, well drained and cut into ½-inch pieces
2	teaspoons Asian sesame oil
2	tablespoons cornstarch
2	tablespoons cold water
	Chopped cilantro or sliced green onions

1. Combine chicken broth, chicken, mushrooms, bamboo shoots, vinegar, soy sauce and chili paste in **CROCK-POT®** slow cooker. Cover and cook on LOW 3 to 4 hours or on HIGH 2 to 3 hours or until done.

2. Stir in tofu and sesame oil. Combine cornstarch with water; mix well. Stir into **CROCK-POT®** slow cooker. Cover and cook on HIGH 10 minutes or until thickened.

3. Garnish with cilantro or green onions.

Campbell's

Campbell's® Asian Tomato Beef

MAKES 8 SERVINGS

PREP TIME: 5 MINUTES
COOK TIME: 7 TO 8 HOURS (LOW) • 4 TO 5 HOURS (HIGH)

2	cans (10¾ ounces each) Campbell's® Tomato Soup
⅓	cup soy sauce
⅓	cup vinegar
1½	teaspoons garlic powder
¼	teaspoon black pepper
3	to 3½ pounds boneless beef round steak, cut into strips
6	cups broccoli flowerets
8	cups hot cooked rice

1. Mix soup, soy, vinegar, garlic, pepper and beef in the **CROCK-POT®** slow cooker. Cover and cook on LOW for 7 to 8 hours or on HIGH 4 to 5 hours or until done.

2. Stir mixture. Add broccoli. Cover and cook on HIGH 15 minutes or until broccoli is tender-crisp. Serve over rice.

Slow-Simmered Curried Chicken

MAKES 4 SERVINGS

PREP TIME: 15 TO 20 MINUTES
COOK TIME: 5 TO 6 HOURS (LOW) • 2 TO 3 HOURS (HIGH)

1½	cups chopped onions
1	medium green bell pepper, chopped
1	pound boneless skinless chicken breast or thighs, cut into bite-size pieces
1	cup medium salsa
2	teaspoons grated fresh ginger
½	teaspoon garlic powder
½	teaspoon red pepper flakes
¼	cup chopped fresh cilantro
1	teaspoon sugar
1	teaspoon curry powder
¾	teaspoon salt
	Hot cooked rice

1. Place onions and bell pepper in bottom of **CROCK-POT®** slow cooker. Top with chicken. Combine salsa, ginger, garlic powder and pepper flakes in small bowl; spoon over chicken. Cover and cook on LOW 5 to 6 hours or on HIGH 2 to 3 hours or until chicken is done.

2. Combine cilantro, sugar, curry powder and salt in small bowl. Stir mixture into **CROCK-POT®** slow cooker. Cover and cook on HIGH 15 minutes or until hot. Serve with rice.

Korean BBQ Beef Short Ribs

MAKES 6 SERVINGS

PREP TIME: 10 TO 15 MINUTES
COOK TIME: 7 TO 8 HOURS (LOW) • 3 TO 4 HOURS (HIGH)

4	to 4½ pounds beef short ribs
¼	cup chopped green onions with tops
¼	cup tamari or soy sauce
¼	cup beef broth or water
1	tablespoon packed brown sugar
2	teaspoons minced fresh ginger
2	teaspoons minced garlic
½	teaspoon black pepper
2	teaspoons Asian sesame oil
	Hot cooked rice or linguine pasta
2	teaspoons sesame seeds, toasted

1. Place ribs in **CROCK-POT®** slow cooker. Combine green onions, soy sauce, broth, brown sugar, ginger, garlic and pepper in medium bowl; mix well and pour over ribs. Cover and cook on LOW 7 to 8 hours or on HIGH 3 to 4 hours or until ribs are fork tender.

2. Remove ribs from cooking liquid, cool slightly. Trim and discard excess fat. Cut rib meat into bite-sized pieces, discarding bones and fat.

3. Let cooking liquid stand 5 minutes to allow fat to rise. Skim off fat and discard.

4. Stir sesame oil into liquid. Return beef to **CROCK-POT®** slow cooker. Cover and cook on LOW 15 to 30 minutes or until mixture is hot. Serve with rice or pasta and garnish with sesame seeds.

Variation: Substitute 3 pounds boneless short ribs for beef short ribs.

Sweet and Sour Shrimp

MAKES 4 TO 6 SERVINGS

PREP TIME: 15 TO 20 MINUTES
COOK TIME: 3 TO 4 HOURS (LOW) • 2 TO 3 HOURS (HIGH)

1	can (16 ounces) sliced peaches in syrup
1	cup chopped onion
1/2	cup chopped red bell pepper
1/2	cup chopped green bell pepper
1/2	cup chopped celery
1/3	cup vegetable broth
2	tablespoons toasted sesame oil
1/4	cup light soy sauce
2	tablespoons rice wine vinegar
1	teaspoon red pepper flakes
6	ounces snow peas
1	pound cooked medium shrimp
1/3	cup chopped toasted almonds

1. Place peaches with syrup, onion, peppers, celery, broth, sesame oil, soy sauce and vinegar in **CROCK-POT®** slow cooker. Cover and cook on LOW 3 to 4 hours or on HIGH 2 to 3 hours or until done. Stir well.

2. Add snow peas. Cook 15 minutes on HIGH. Add shrimp and almonds. Cook 4 to 5 minutes on HIGH or until shrimp are hot. Serve with rice.

Spicy Asian Pork Filling

MAKES 20 (¼-CUP) SERVINGS

PREP TIME: 15 TO 20 MINUTES
COOK TIME: 8 TO 10 HOURS (LOW) • 4 TO 5 HOURS (HIGH)

1   **(3-pound) boneless pork sirloin roast, cut into 2- to 3-inch chunks**
½   **cup tamari or soy sauce**
1   **tablespoon chili garlic sauce or chili paste**
2   **teaspoons minced fresh ginger**
2   **tablespoons water**
1   **tablespoon cornstarch**
2   **teaspoons dark sesame oil**

1. Combine pork, tamari, chili garlic sauce and ginger in **CROCK-POT®** slow cooker; mix well. Cover and cook on LOW 8 to 10 hours or on HIGH 4 to 5 hours or until pork is fork tender.

2. Remove roast from cooking liquid; cool slightly. Trim and discard excess fat. Shred pork using 2 forks. Let cooking liquid stand 5 minutes to allow fat to rise. Skim off and discard fat.

3. Blend water, cornstarch and sesame oil; whisk into cooking liquid. Cook on HIGH until thickened. Add shredded meat to **CROCK-POT®** slow cooker; mix well. Cook 15 to 30 minutes or until hot.

Variations: Spicy Asian Pork Bundles: Place ¼ cup pork filling into large lettuce leaves. Wrap to enclose. Makes about 20 bundles.

Moo Shu Pork: Lightly spread plum sauce over warm small flour tortillas. Spoon ¼ cup pork filling and ¼ cup stir-fried vegetables into tortillas. Wrap to enclose. Serve immediately. Makes about 20 wraps.

TENDER SLOW-COOKED
BARBECUE AND SPICY CHILI,
SO EASY TO PREPARE

Casual
CHILI & BBQ
and More

Bean and Corn Chili

MAKES 6 SERVINGS

PREP TIME: 15 TO 20 MINUTES
COOK TIME: 6 TO 8 HOURS (LOW) • 3 TO 4 HOURS (HIGH)

2	medium onions, finely chopped
5	cloves garlic, minced
2	tablespoons red wine
½	teaspoon olive oil
1½	cups nonfat chicken or vegetable broth
1	green bell pepper, seeded and finely chopped
1	red bell pepper, seeded and finely chopped
1	stalk celery, finely sliced
6	Roma tomatoes, chopped
2	cans (15 ounces each) kidney beans, rinsed and drained
1	can (6 ounces) tomato paste
1	cup frozen corn kernels
1	teaspoon salt
1	teaspoon chili powder
½	teaspoon black pepper
¼	teaspoon cumin
¼	teaspoon ground red pepper
¼	teaspoon dried oregano
¼	teaspoon ground coriander

Cook onions and garlic in wine and oil in medium skillet. Transfer to
CROCK-POT® slow cooker. Add broth, bell peppers, celery, tomatoes, beans,
tomato paste, corn, salt, chili powder, black pepper, cumin, red pepper,
oregano and coriander; mix well. Cover and cook on LOW 6 to 8 hours or on
HIGH 3 to 4 hours or until done.

Rio Grande Ribs

MAKES 6 SERVINGS

PREP TIME: 15 MINUTES
COOK TIME: 6 HOURS (LOW) • 3 HOURS (HIGH)

4	pounds country-style pork ribs, trimmed of all visible fat
	Salt, to taste
	Black pepper, to taste
1	jar (16 ounces) picante sauce
½	cup beer, nonalcoholic malt beverage or beef broth
¼	cup **Frank's® RedHot®** Cayenne Pepper Sauce
1	teaspoon chili powder
2	cups **French's®** French Fried Onions

1. Season ribs with salt and pepper. Broil ribs 6 inches from heat on rack in broiler pan for 10 minutes or until well-browned, turning once. Place ribs in the **CROCK-POT®** slow cooker. Combine picante sauce, beer, **Frank's® RedHot®** Cayenne Pepper Sauce and chili powder in small bowl. Pour mixture over top.

2. Cover and cook on LOW for 6 hours or on HIGH for 3 hours or until ribs are tender. Transfer ribs to serving platter; keep warm. Skim fat from liquid.

3. Turn the **CROCK-POT®** slow cooker to HIGH. Add 1 cup **French's®** French Fried Onions to the stoneware. Cook 10 to 15 minutes or until slightly thickened. Spoon sauce over ribs and sprinkle with remaining 1 cup **French's®** French Fried Onions. Splash on more **Frank's® RedHot®** Cayenne Pepper Sauce to taste.

Tip: Prepare ingredients the night before for quick assembly in the morning. Keep refrigerated until ready to cook.

BUSH's® BEST 3-Bean Chili

MAKES 8 SERVINGS

PREP TIME: 15 MINUTES
COOK TIME: 3 TO 4 HOURS (LOW) • 2 TO 3 HOURS (HIGH)

2	pounds lean ground round beef
3	teaspoons chili powder
1	small yellow onion, chopped
1	small green bell pepper, seeded and chopped
2	cans (16 ounces) BUSH's® BEST Dark Red Kidney Beans
2	cans (16 ounces) BUSH's® BEST Pinto Beans
2	cans (15 ounces) BUSH's® BEST Black Beans
1	can (14½ ounces) diced tomatoes
1	can (6 ounces) tomato paste
1½	teaspoons salt
1	teaspoon garlic salt
½	teaspoon black pepper
½	teaspoon ground cumin
⅛	teaspoon ground cinnamon
	Sour cream (optional)

1. Brown ground beef in large skillet. Drain excess fat and scrape contents of skillet into the **CROCK-POT®** slow cooker. Add chili powder, onion, green pepper, beans, tomatoes, tomato paste, salt, garlic salt, black pepper, cumin and cinnamon.

2. Cover and cook on LOW for 3 to 4 hours or on HIGH for 2 to 3 hours.

3. Garnish with sour cream, if desired.

CASUAL CHILI & BBQ

McCormick® Weeknight Chili

MAKES 4 SERVINGS

PREP TIME: 5 MINUTES
COOK TIME: 1 TO 2 HOURS (LOW) • 1 HOUR (HIGH)

1   **pound ground beef or ground turkey**
2   **cans (8 ounces each) tomato sauce**
1   **can (15 ounces) red kidney beans, undrained**
1   **package (1¼ ounces) McCormick® Chili Seasoning**
1   **cup shredded Cheddar cheese**
    Chopped onion (optional)

1. Cook ground beef or turkey in a 12-inch skillet until no longer pink, stirring often; drain.

2. Scrape contents of skillet into **CROCK-POT®** slow cooker. Stir in tomato sauce, beans and seasoning. Cover and cook on LOW for 1 to 2 hours or cook on HIGH for 45 minutes to 1 hour, or until done.

3. Stir chili before serving. Top with cheese and onion, if desired.

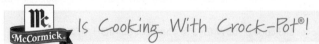

Is Cooking With Crock-Pot®!

For an American regional twist, try making this chili Cincinnati style! Just add 1 teaspoon **McCormick® Ground Cinnamon** and serve the chili over boiled macaroni elbow noodles.

Barbecued Pulled Pork Sandwiches

MAKES 8 SERVINGS

PREP TIME: 15 TO 20 MINUTES
COOK TIME: 12 TO 14 HOURS (LOW) • 6 TO 7 HOURS (HIGH)

1   pork shoulder roast (about 2½ pounds)
1   bottle (14 ounces) barbecue sauce
1   tablespoon fresh lemon juice
1   teaspoon brown sugar
1   medium onion, chopped
8   hamburger buns or hard rolls

1. Place pork roast in **CROCK-POT**® slow cooker. Cover and cook on LOW 10 to 12 hours or on HIGH 5 to 6 hours or until done.

2. Remove pork roast from **CROCK-POT**® slow cooker; discard cooking liquid. Shred pork with 2 forks. Return pork to **CROCK-POT**® slow cooker. Add barbecue sauce, lemon juice, brown sugar and onion. Cover and cook on LOW 2 hours or on HIGH for 1 hour.

3. Serve shredded pork on hamburger buns or hard rolls.

Note: For a 5-, 6- or 7-quart **CROCK-POT**® slow cooker, double all ingredients, except barbecue sauce. Increase barbecue sauce to 21 ounces.

Sweet & Saucy Ribs

MAKES 4 SERVINGS

PREP TIME: 20 TO 25 MINUTES
COOK TIME: 6 TO 8 HOURS (LOW) • 3 TO 4 HOURS (HIGH)

2	pounds pork baby back ribs
1	teaspoon black pepper
2½	cups barbecue sauce (not mesquite-flavored)
1	jar (8 ounces) cherry jam or preserves
1	tablespoon Dijon mustard
¼	teaspoon salt
	Salt (optional)
	Black pepper (optional)

1. Trim and discard excess fat from ribs. Rub 1 teaspoon black pepper over ribs. Cut ribs into 2-rib portions; place in **CROCK-POT**® slow cooker.

2. Combine barbecue sauce, jam, mustard and salt in small bowl; pour over ribs. Cover and cook on LOW 6 to 8 hours or HIGH 3 to 4 hours or until ribs are tender.

3. Taste and adjust seasonings with additional salt and pepper, if desired. Serve ribs with sauce.

Campbell's® Hearty Beef & Bean Chili

MAKES 6 SERVINGS

PREP TIME: 10 MINUTES
COOK TIME: 8 TO 10 HOURS (LOW) • 4 TO 5 HOURS (HIGH)

1½	**pounds ground beef**
1	**large onion, chopped**
2	**cloves garlic, minced**
1	**can (10¾ ounces) Campbell's® Tomato Soup**
1	**can (14½ ounces) diced tomatoes**
½	**cup water**
2	**cans (about 15 ounces each) red kidney beans**
¼	**cup chili powder**
2	**teaspoons ground cumin**

1. Cook beef in skillet until browned. Pour off fat.

2. Mix beef, onion, garlic, soup, tomatoes, water, beans, chili powder and cumin in **CROCK-POT®** slow cooker.

3. Cover and cook on LOW for 8 to 10 hours or on HIGH for 4 to 5 hours or until done.

Barbecued Beef Sandwiches

MAKES 12 SERVINGS

PREP TIME: 20 TO 25 MINUTES
COOK TIME: 8 TO 10 HOURS (LOW) • 4 TO 5 HOURS (HIGH)

3	pounds boneless beef chuck shoulder roast
2	cups ketchup
1	medium onion, chopped
¼	cup cider vinegar
¼	cup dark molasses
2	tablespoons Worcestershire sauce
2	cloves garlic, minced
½	teaspoon salt
½	teaspoon dry mustard
½	teaspoon black pepper
¼	teaspoon garlic powder
¼	teaspoon red pepper flakes
	Sesame seed buns, split

1. Cut roast in half and place into **CROCK-POT®** slow cooker. Combine ketchup, onion, vinegar, molasses, Worcestershire sauce, garlic, salt, mustard, black pepper, garlic powder and red pepper flakes in large bowl. Pour sauce mixture over roast. Cover and cook on LOW 8 to 10 hours or on HIGH 4 to 5 hours or until done.

2. Remove roast from cooking liquid; cool slightly. Trim and discard excess fat from beef. Shred meat with 2 forks.

3. Let cooking liquid stand 5 minutes to allow fat to rise. Skim off and discard fat.

4. Return meat to **CROCK-POT®** slow cooker. Stir to evenly coat meat with sauce. Adjust seasonings. Cover and cook on LOW 15 to 30 minutes or until hot.

5. Spoon filling into sandwich buns and top with additional barbecue sauce, if desired.

American
CLASSICS

Pork Loin with Sherry and Red Onions

MAKES 8 SERVINGS

PREP TIME: 15 MINUTES
COOK TIME: 8 TO 10 HOURS (LOW) • 5 TO 6 HOURS (HIGH)

3	large red onions, thinly sliced
1	cup pearl onions, blanched and peeled
1	tablespoon unsalted butter or margarine
1	boneless pork loin, tied (about $2\frac{1}{2}$ pounds)
$\frac{1}{2}$	teaspoon salt
$\frac{1}{2}$	teaspoon freshly ground black pepper
$\frac{1}{2}$	cup cooking sherry
1	tablespoon chopped Italian parsley
$1\frac{1}{2}$	tablespoons cornstarch
2	tablespoons water

1. Cook red onion and pearl onions in butter in medium skillet until soft.

2. Rub pork loin with salt and pepper and place in **CROCK-POT®** slow cooker. Add cooked onions, sherry and parsley. Cover and cook on LOW 8 to 10 hours or on HIGH 5 to 6 hours or until done.

3. Remove pork loin from **CROCK-POT®** slow cooker and let stand 15 minutes before slicing.

4. Combine cornstarch and water. Add to cooking liquid in **CROCK-POT®** slow cooker, stirring to thicken sauce. Serve pork loin with onions and sherry sauce.

Swanson® Beef & Vegetable Soup

MAKES 6 SERVINGS

PREP TIME: 25 MINUTES
COOK TIME: 8 TO 10 HOURS • 4 TO 5 HOURS

1	pound boneless beef stew meat, cut into 1-inch cubes
2	tablespoons all-purpose flour
2	tablespoons vegetable oil
3	large onions, chopped
12	small red-skinned potatoes, cut into quarters
2	medium carrots, sliced
4	cloves garlic, minced
1	tablespoon chopped fresh thyme or 1 teaspoon dried thyme leaves, crushed
2	tablespoons tomato paste
1½	teaspoons instant coffee crystals
1	carton (32 ounces) Swanson® Beef Broth
	Sour cream (optional)
	Chopped green onions (optional)

1. Season beef with pepper and coat with flour.

2. Heat oil in skillet. Add beef and cook until browned.

3. Place onions, potatoes, carrots, garlic and thyme in the **CROCK-POT®** slow cooker. Top with browned beef. Mix tomato paste, coffee and 1 cup broth. Pour coffee mixture and remaining broth into the **CROCK-POT®** slow cooker.

4. Cover and cook on LOW for 8 to 10 hours or on HIGH for 4 to 5 hours or until done.

5. Serve with sour cream and chopped green onions if desired.

Cheesy Broccoli Casserole

MAKES 4 TO 6 SERVINGS

PREP TIME: 5 TO 10 MINUTES
COOK TIME: 5 TO 6 HOURS (LOW) • 2½ TO 3 HOURS (HIGH)

2	packages (10 ounces each) chopped broccoli, thawed
1	can (10¾ ounces) condensed cream of celery soup
1¼	cups shredded sharp Cheddar cheese, divided
¼	cup minced onions
1	teaspoon paprika
1	teaspoon hot pepper sauce
½	teaspoon celery seed
1	cup crushed potato chips or saltine crackers

1. Lightly coat **CROCK-POT®** slow cooker with nonstick cooking spray. Combine broccoli, soup, 1 cup cheese, onions, paprika, pepper sauce and celery seed in **CROCK-POT®** slow cooker; mix thoroughly. Cover and cook on LOW 5 to 6 hours or on HIGH 2½ to 3 hours or until done.

2. Uncover; sprinkle top with potato chips and remaining ¼ cup cheese. Cook, uncovered, on LOW 30 to 60 minutes or on HIGH 15 to 30 minutes or until cheese melts.

 Tip

For a change in taste, prepare this dish with thawed chopped spinach, and top with crushed crackers or spicy croutons to create the cheesy crust!

Fresh Herbed Turkey Breast

MAKES 8 SERVINGS

PREP TIME: 5 MINUTES
COOK TIME: 8 TO 10 HOURS (LOW) • 4 TO 5 HOURS (HIGH)

¼	**cup minced fresh sage**
¼	**cup minced fresh tarragon**
⅛	**cup butter, softened**
1	**clove garlic, minced**
1	**teaspoon black pepper**
½	**teaspoon salt**
1	**split turkey breast (about 4 pounds)**
1½	**tablespoons cornstarch**

1. Combine sage, tarragon, butter, garlic, pepper and salt. Rub mixture all over turkey breast.

2. Place turkey breast in **CROCK-POT®** slow cooker. Cover and cook on LOW 8 to 10 hours or on HIGH 4 to 5 hours or until done.

3. Transfer turkey breast to cutting board. Increase heat on **CROCK-POT®** slow cooker to HIGH. Slowly mix cornstarch into cooking liquid with whisk. When sauce is thick and smooth, pour over turkey breast. Slice to serve.

Spinach Gorgonzola Corn Bread

MAKES 10 TO 12 SERVINGS

PREP TIME: 8 MINUTES • COOK TIME: 1 ½ HOURS (HIGH)

- **2** boxes (8½ ounces each) corn bread mix
- **3** eggs
- **½** cup cream
- **1** box (10 ounces) frozen chopped spinach, thawed and drained
- **1** cup crumbled gorgonzola cheese
- **1** teaspoon ground black pepper
  Paprika (optional)

Coat **CROCK-POT®** slow cooker with nonstick cooking spray. Mix all ingredients in medium bowl. Pour batter into **CROCK-POT®** slow cooker. Cover and cook on HIGH 1½ hours. Sprinkle top with paprika for more colorful crust, if desired. Let bread cool completely before inverting onto serving platter.

Note: Cook only on HIGH setting for proper crust and texture.

Swanson® Hearty Beef Stew

MAKES 6 SERVINGS

PREP TIME: 20 MINUTES
COOK TIME: 10 TO 12 HOURS (LOW) • 4 TO 5 HOURS (HIGH)

1½	**pounds beef stew meat, cut into cubes**
¼	**cup all-purpose flour, divided**
1	**tablespoon vegetable oil**
2½	**cups cubed potatoes**
4	**medium carrots, sliced (about 2 cups)**
2	**medium onions, cut into wedges**
4	**cloves garlic, minced**
1	**tablespoon Worcestershire sauce**
1	**teaspoon dried thyme leaves, crushed**
1	**bay leaf**
3	**cups Swanson® Beef Broth**
¼	**cup water**
1	**cup frozen peas**

1. Season beef with pepper and coat with 2 tablespoons flour. Heat oil in skillet. Add beef and cook until browned.

2. Place potatoes, carrots, onions and garlic in the **CROCK-POT®** slow cooker. Top with beef. Add Worcestershire, thyme, bay leaf and broth.

3. Cover and cook on LOW for 10 to 12 hours or on HIGH for 4 to 5 hours or until done. Remove bay leaf.

4. Mix remaining flour and water. Add peas and flour mixture to **CROCK-POT®** slow cooker. Cook on HIGH 15 minutes or until slightly thickened.

Is Cooking With Crock-Pot®!

Freeze leftovers of this hearty stew as individual portions; just reheat in a microwave for fast weeknight dinners!

Campbell's® Lemon Chicken

MAKES 8 SERVINGS

PREP TIME: 5 MINUTES
COOK TIME: 7 TO 8 HOURS (LOW) • 4 TO 5 HOURS (HIGH)

2	cans (10¾ ounces each) Campbell's® Cream of Chicken or 98% Fat Free Cream of Chicken Soup
½	cup water
¼	cup lemon juice
1	tablespoon Dijon mustard
1½	teaspoons garlic powder
8	large carrots, thickly sliced
8	boneless chicken breast halves
8	cups hot cooked egg noodles
	Chopped fresh parsley

1. Mix the soup, water, lemon juice, mustard, garlic and carrots in the **CROCK-POT®** slow cooker. Add chicken and turn to coat.

2. Cover and cook on LOW for 7 to 8 hours or on HIGH for 4 to 5 hours or until done.

3. Serve over noodles and sprinkle with parsley.

Jambalaya

MAKES 6 SERVINGS

PREP TIME: 10 MINUTES
COOK TIME: 6 TO 7 HOURS (LOW) • 3½ TO 4 HOURS (HIGH)

2½	to 3 pounds chicken pieces, skinned if desired
1	can (14½ ounces) diced tomatoes
1	can (14½ ounces) chicken broth
1	green bell pepper, chopped
2	cups **French's®** French Fried Onions
¼	cup **Frank's® RedHot®** Cayenne Pepper Sauce
2	cloves garlic, chopped
2	teaspoons Old Bay® seafood seasoning
1½	teaspoons dried oregano leaves
¾	teaspoon salt
½	teaspoon ground black pepper
1	cup uncooked regular rice
1	pound shrimp, peeled and deveined

1. Combine the chicken, tomatoes, chicken broth, green pepper, 1 cup **French's®** French Fried Onions, **Frank's® RedHot®** Cayenne Pepper Sauce, garlic, seafood seasoning, oregano, salt and pepper in the **CROCK-POT®** slow cooker. Cover and cook on LOW for 4 to 5 hours or on HIGH for 2 to 2½ hours.

2. Stir in the rice. Cook on LOW for 2 hours or on HIGH for 1 hour or until rice is cooked and all liquid is absorbed.

3. Turn **CROCK-POT®** slow cooker to HIGH. Add shrimp. Cover and cook 30 minutes or until shrimp are no longer pink. Arrange jambalaya on serving platter. Sprinkle with remaining **French's®** French Fried Onions.

Campbell's® Autumn Beef Pot Roast au Jus

MAKES 6 SERVINGS

PREP TIME: 10 MINUTES
COOK TIME: 10 TO 12 HOURS (LOW) • 4 TO 5 HOURS (HIGH)

- **4** cups peeled sweet potatoes cut in 1¼-inch chunks (about 1½ pounds)
- **1** medium onion, coarsely chopped
- **2** medium Granny Smith apples, cored and each cut into 12 wedges
- **1** can (10½ ounces) Campbell's® Condensed Beef Broth
- **2** teaspoons dried thyme leaves, crushed
- **2** pounds boneless beef chuck roast

1. Place sweet potatoes, onion, apples, broth and thyme in the **CROCK-POT®** slow cooker. Add roast.

2. Cover and cook on LOW for 10 to 12 hours or on HIGH 4 to 5 hours or until done.

Campbell's Is Cooking With Crock-Pot®!

You may substitute or use a combination of medium red potatoes and peeled sweet potatoes cut into 1¼-inch chunks.

Campbell's® Savory Pot Roast

MAKES 7 TO 8 SERVINGS

PREP TIME: 10 MINUTES
COOK TIME: 8 TO 9 HOURS (LOW) • 4 TO 5 HOURS (HIGH)

1   can (10¾ ounces) Campbell's® Cream of Mushroom or
     98% Fat Free Cream of Mushroom Soup
1   pouch dry onion soup mix
6   medium potatoes, cut into 1-inch pieces
6   medium carrots, thickly sliced
1   (3½- to 4-pound) boneless beef chuck roast

1. Mix the soup, soup mix, potatoes and carrots in the **CROCK-POT**® slow cooker. Add the roast and turn to coat.

2. Cover and cook on LOW for 8 to 9 hours or on HIGH for 4 to 5 hours or until done.

Campbell's® Creamy Chicken & Wild Rice

MAKES 8 SERVINGS

PREP TIME: 5 MINUTES
COOK TIME: 7 TO 8 HOURS (LOW) • 4 TO 5 HOURS (HIGH)

- **2** cans ($10\frac{3}{4}$ ounces each) Campbell's® Cream of Chicken or 98% Fat Free Cream of Chicken Soup
- **1½** cups water
- **1** package (6 ounces) seasoned long-grain and wild rice mix
- **4** large carrots, thickly sliced
- **8** boneless chicken breast halves

1. Mix the soup, water, rice and carrots in the **CROCK-POT®** slow cooker. Add chicken and turn to coat.

2. Cover and cook on LOW for 7 to 8 hours or on HIGH for 4 to 5 hours or until done.

Campbell's® Golden Mushroom Pork & Apples

MAKES 8 SERVINGS

PREP TIME: 10 MINUTES
COOK TIME: 8 TO 9 HOURS (LOW) • 4 TO 5 HOURS (HIGH)

- 2 cans (11¾ ounces each) Campbell's® Golden Mushroom Soup
- ½ cup water
- 1 tablespoon brown sugar
- 1 tablespoon Worcestershire sauce
- 1 teaspoon dried thyme leaves, crushed
- 4 large Granny Smith apples, sliced
- 2 large onions, sliced
- 8 boneless pork chops, ¾ inch thick

1. Mix the soup, water, brown sugar, Worcestershire and thyme in the **CROCK-POT®** slow cooker. Add apples, onions and pork.

2. Cover and cook on LOW 8 to 9 hours or on HIGH 4 to 5 hours or until done.

Campbell's® Apricot Glazed Pork Roast

MAKES 8 SERVINGS

PREP TIME: 5 MINUTES
COOK TIME: 8 TO 9 HOURS (LOW) • 4 TO 5 HOURS (HIGH)

1	**can (10½ ounces) Campbell's® Condensed Chicken Broth**
1	**jar (18 ounces) apricot preserves**
1	**large onion, chopped**
2	**tablespoons Dijon mustard**
1	**(3½- to 4-pound) boneless pork loin roast**

1. Mix broth, preserves, onion and mustard in the **CROCK-POT®** slow cooker. Cut pork roast to fit and add to the **CROCK-POT®** slow cooker.

2. Cover and cook on LOW for 8 to 9 hours or on HIGH for 4 to 5 hours or until done.

Tip: For thicker sauce, mix together 2 tablespoons cornstarch and 2 tablespoons water. Remove pork from the **CROCK-POT®** slow cooker. Stir cornstarch mixture into the **CROCK-POT®** slow cooker. Cover and cook on HIGH for 10 minutes or until mixture boils and thickens.

Cajun Chicken and Shrimp Creole

MAKES 6 SERVINGS

PREP TIME: 12 TO 15 MINUTES
COOK TIME: 8 TO 10 HOURS (LOW) • 4 TO 5 HOURS (HIGH)

1   **pound boneless skinless chicken thighs**
1   **red bell pepper, chopped**
1   **large onion, chopped**
1   **stalk celery, diced**
1   **can (15 ounces) stewed tomatoes, undrained and chopped**
1   **clove garlic, minced**
1   **tablespoon sugar**
1   **teaspoon paprika**
1   **teaspoon Cajun seasoning**
1   **teaspoon salt**
1   **teaspoon black pepper**
1   **pound shrimp, peeled, deveined and cleaned**
1   **tablespoon fresh lemon juice**
     Louisiana-style hot sauce, to taste
     Hot cooked rice

1. Place chicken in **CROCK-POT®** slow cooker. Add bell pepper, onion, celery, tomatoes, garlic, sugar, paprika, Cajun seasoning, salt and pepper. Cover and cook on LOW 7 to 9 hours or on HIGH 3 to 4 hours.

2. Add shrimp, lemon juice and hot sauce. Cover and cook 45 minutes to 1 hour or until shrimp are done. Serve over hot rice.

Sweet Sips &
DESSERTS

Brownie Bottoms

MAKES 6 SERVINGS

PREP TIME: 12 MINUTES
COOK TIME: 1½ HOURS (HIGH)

¾	cup water
½	cup firmly packed brown sugar
2	tablespoons unsweetened cocoa powder
2½	cups packaged brownie mix
1	package (2¾ ounces) instant chocolate pudding mix
½	cup milk chocolate chip morsels
2	eggs, beaten
3	tablespoons butter or margarine, melted
	Whipped cream or ice cream (optional)

1. Lightly coat **CROCK-POT**® slow cooker with nonstick cooking spray; set aside. Combine water, brown sugar and cocoa powder in a small saucepan, and bring to a boil.

2. Combine brownie mix, pudding mix, chocolate chips, eggs and butter in medium bowl; stir until well blended. Spread batter in **CROCK-POT**® slow cooker. Pour boiling mixture over batter. Cover and cook on HIGH 1½ hours.

3. Turn off **CROCK-POT**® slow cooker and let stand 30 minutes. Serve warm with whipped cream or ice cream, if desired.

Homestyle Apple Brown Betty

MAKES 8 SERVINGS

PREP TIME: 15 MINUTES
COOK TIME: 3 TO 4 HOURS (LOW) • 2 HOURS (HIGH)

- 6   cups of your favorite cooking apples, peeled, cored and cut into eighths
- 1   cup bread crumbs
- ¾   cup firmly packed brown sugar
- ½   cup butter or margarine, melted
- ¼   cup walnuts, finely chopped
- 1   teaspoon ground cinnamon
- 1   teaspoon ground nutmeg
- ⅛   teaspoon salt

1. Lightly coat **CROCK-POT®** slow cooker with nonstick cooking spray. Place apples in bottom.

2. Combine bread crumbs, brown sugar, butter, walnuts, cinnamon, nutmeg and salt in mixing bowl. Spread mixture over apples.

3. Cover and cook on LOW 3 to 4 hours or on HIGH 2 hours or until done.

Mulled Cranberry Tea

MAKES 8 SERVINGS

PREP TIME: 10 MINUTES
COOK TIME: 2 TO 3 HOURS (LOW) • 1 TO 2 HOURS (HIGH)

2   **tea bags**
1   **cup boiling water**
1   **bottle (48 ounces) cranberry juice**
½   **cup dried cranberries (optional)**
⅓   **cup sugar**
1   **large lemon, cut into ¼-inch slices**
4   **cinnamon sticks**
6   **whole cloves**
     Additional thin lemon slices
     Additional cinnamon sticks

1. Place tea bags in **CROCK-POT®** slow cooker. Pour boiling water over tea bags; cover and let stand 5 minutes. Remove and discard tea bags.

2. Add cranberry juice, cranberries, if desired, sugar, lemon slices, cinnamon sticks and cloves. Cover and cook on LOW 2 to 3 hours or HIGH 1 to 2 hours or until done.

3. Remove and discard lemon slices, cinnamon sticks and cloves. Serve in warm mugs with additional fresh lemon slices and cinnamon sticks.

Steamed Pumpkin Cake

MAKES 12 SERVINGS

PREP TIME: 15 MINUTES • COOK TIME: 3 TO 3½ HOURS (HIGH)

1½	**cups all-purpose flour**
1½	**teaspoons baking powder**
1½	**teaspoons baking soda**
1	**teaspoon ground cinnamon**
½	**teaspoon salt**
¼	**teaspoon ground cloves**
½	**cup unsalted butter, melted**
2	**cups packed light brown sugar**
3	**eggs, beaten**
1	**can (15 ounces) pumpkin purée**
	Sweetened whipped cream (optional)

1. Grease 2½-quart soufflé dish or baking pan that fits into **CROCK-POT**® slow cooker; set aside. Combine flour, baking powder, baking soda, cinnamon, salt and cloves in medium bowl; set aside.

2. Beat butter, brown sugar and eggs in large bowl with electric mixer on medium speed until creamy. Beat in pumpkin. Stir in flour mixture. Spoon batter into prepared soufflé dish.

3. Fill **CROCK-POT**® slow cooker with 1 inch hot water. Prepare foil handles (see below). Place soufflé dish into **CROCK-POT**® slow cooker. Cover and cook on HIGH 3 to 3½ hours or until wooden toothpick inserted into center comes out clean.

4. Use foil handles to lift dish from **CROCK-POT**® slow cooker. Cool 15 minutes. Invert cake onto serving platter. Cut into wedges and serve with dollop of whipped cream, if desired.

Foil handles: Tear off three 18×2-inch strips of heavy foil or use regular foil folded to double thickness. Crisscross foil strips in spoke design and place into **CROCK-POT**® slow cooker. Place soufflé dish in center of strips. Pull foil strips up and over dish.

Serving suggestion: Top with cooked apple or pear slices, or a scoop of ice cream.

Banana Nut Bread

MAKES 6 SERVINGS

PREP TIME: 15 MINUTES • COOK TIME: 1¼ TO 1½ HOURS (HIGH)

1¾	cups all-purpose flour, sifted
2	teaspoons baking powder
½	teaspoon salt
¼	teaspoon baking soda
⅓	cup butter or margarine
⅔	cup granulated sugar
2	eggs, well beaten
2	tablespoons dark corn syrup
3	ripe bananas, well mashed
½	cup chopped walnuts

1. Grease and flour **CROCK-POT®** slow cooker; set aside. Sift together flour, baking powder, salt and baking soda in small bowl; set aside.

2. Cream butter in large bowl with electric mixer at medium-high speed until fluffy. Slowly add sugar, eggs, corn syrup and mashed bananas. Beat until smooth. Gradually add flour mixture to creamed mixture. Add walnuts and mix well. Pour into **CROCK-POT®** slow cooker. Cover and cook on HIGH 1¼ to 1½ hours or until toothpick inserted into center comes out clean.

3. Let cool, then invert bread onto serving platter.

Cran-Apple Orange Conserve

MAKES ABOUT 5 CUPS (¼ CUP PER SERVING)

PREP TIME: 12 MINUTES
COOK TIME: 6 HOURS (LOW) • 3 TO 3½ HOURS (HIGH)

2 **medium oranges**
5 **large tart apples, peeled, cored and chopped**
2 **cups sugar**
1½ **cups fresh cranberries**
1 **tablespoon grated fresh lemon peel**

1. Remove thin slice from both ends of both oranges for easier chopping. Finely chop unpeeled oranges and remove any seeds. You should have about 2 cups of chopped oranges.

2. Combine chopped oranges, apples, sugar, cranberries and lemon peel in **CROCK-POT®** slow cooker. Cover and cook on LOW 4 hours or on HIGH 2 hours.

3. Slightly crush fruit with potato masher. Cook, uncovered, on LOW 2 hours or on HIGH 1 to 1½ hours longer or until very thick, stirring occasionally to prevent sticking. Cool at least 2 hours.

4. Serve with waffles, pancakes or pound cake.

Serving suggestion: Fruit conserve can also be served with roast pork or poultry.

Index

Acknowledgments

The publisher would like to thank the companies listed below for the
use of their recipes and photographs in this publication.

Bush Brothers & Company
Campbell® Soup Company
McCormick Delaware, Inc.
Reckitt Benckiser Inc.